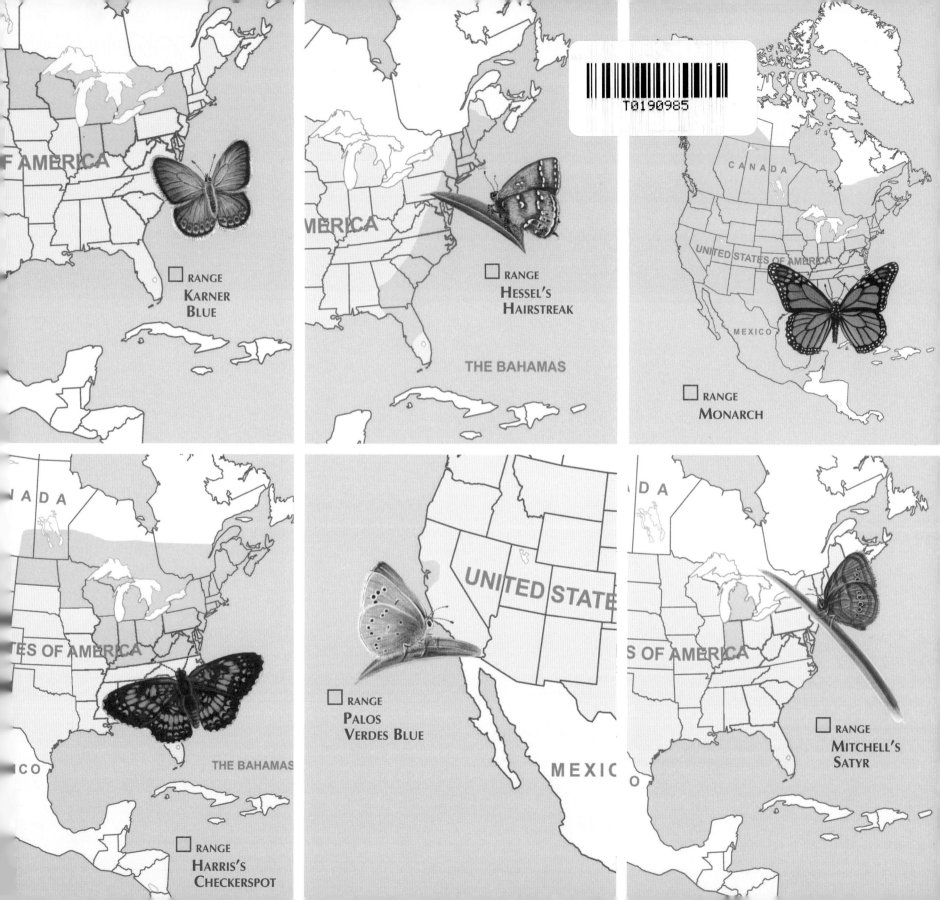

RANGE
KARNER BLUE

RANGE
HESSEL'S HAIRSTREAK

THE BAHAMAS

RANGE
MONARCH

RANGE
HARRIS'S CHECKERSPOT

THE BAHAMAS

RANGE
PALOS VERDES BLUE

RANGE
MITCHELL'S SATYR

CANADA

UNITED STATES OF AMERICA

MEXICO

T0190985

A PLACE FOR
BUTTERFLIES

For Colin, Claire, and Caroline

—M. S.

For my new grandchild,
Andrew Jordan Bond:
welcome to the world!

—H. B.

Published by
PEACHTREE PUBLISHING COMPANY INC.
1700 Chattahoochee Avenue
Atlanta, Georgia 30318-2112
PeachtreeBooks.com

Book design by Loraine M. Joyner
Composition by Melanie McMahon Ives
Illustrations created in acrylic on cold press illustration board.
Title typeset in Hardlyworthit; main text typeset in Monotype's Century Schoolbook with Optima initial capitals. Sidebars typeset in Optima.

Printed and bound in April 2024 at Toppan Leefung, DongGuan, China.
10 9 8 7 6 5 4 3 2 1 (hardcover)
30 29 28 27 26 25 24 (trade paperback)
Third Edition

HC ISBN: 978-1-68263-663-3
PB ISBN: 978-1-56145-784-7

Library of Congress Cataloging-in-Publication Data

Names: Stewart, Melissa, author. | Bond, Higgins, illustrator.
Title: A place for butterflies / written by Melissa Stewart ; illustrated by Higgins Bond.
Description: Third edition. | Atlanta, Georgia : Peachtree Publishing Company Inc., 2024. | Series: A place for. . . | Includes bibliographical references. | Audience: Ages 7 - 11 | Audience: Grades 2-3 | Summary: "The latest updated edition of this fact-filled, colorful look at the amazing world of butterflies, which includes two brand new illustrations and a call to action to protect these creatures and their habitats"-- Provided by publisher.
Identifiers: LCCN 2023054923 | ISBN 9781682636633 (hc) | ISBN 9781561457847
    (pb) | ISBN 9781682636800 (ebook)
Subjects: LCSH: Butterflies--Ecology--Juvenile literature. | Butterflies--Effect of human beings on--Juvenile literature. | CYAC: Butterflies.
Classification: LCC QL544.2 .S746 2024 | DDC 595.78/9--dc23/eng/20240208
LC record available at *https://lccn.loc.gov/2023054923*

A PLACE FOR
BUTTERFLIES

Written by
Melissa Stewart

Illustrated by
Higgins Bond

PEACHTREE
ATLANTA

Butterflies fill our world with beauty and grace. But sometimes people do things that make it hard for them to live and grow.

If we work together to help these special insects, there will always be a place for butterflies.

A BUTTERFLY'S LIFE

As butterflies grow, they go through four life stages. A female butterfly lays her eggs on plants. When an egg hatches, a caterpillar wriggles out. After a few weeks of nonstop eating, the caterpillar becomes a pupa. It is surrounded by a hard chrysalis. When the chrysalis splits open, a winged adult enters the world.

egg

caterpillar

pupa

adult black swallowtail

Like all living things, butterflies need to eat certain foods. Many adult butterflies feed on flower nectar.

EASTERN TIGER SWALLOWTAIL

Have you ever seen an eastern tiger swallowtail fluttering around a wildflower garden or resting on an apple tree? These butterflies spend their days sipping sweet nectar. Their favorite flowers include lilacs, apple blossoms, and wild cherry blossoms. When people grow trees and other flowering plants in their yards, eastern tiger swallowtail butterflies have plenty of food.

When people have gardens in their yards, butterflies can live and grow.

Some butterflies feed on sugary tree sap.

When people work to protect forests, butterflies can live and grow.

MOURNING CLOAK

Most butterflies feed on nectar, but mourning cloaks sip tree sap and juices from rotting fruit. When wooded areas are destroyed to make room for houses and other buildings, mourning cloaks have trouble surviving. When people protect and preserve forests, mourning cloaks have a place to live and food to eat.

Many caterpillars eat only one kind of plant. Some caterpillars depend on plants that grow on burned land.

KARNER BLUE

We think of wildfires as dangerous and destructive, but Karner blue caterpillars depend on them to survive. The caterpillars eat only wild lupine, a plant that grows best in places where other plants have been burned away. At sites in New Hampshire and New York, people carefully set fires to create the perfect habitat for Karner blues. Thanks to their hard work, the number of butterflies is growing.

When people let some wildfires burn, butterflies can live and grow.

Other caterpillars depend on trees that grow in freshwater swamps near the ocean. As global warming causes ice caps to melt and sea levels to rise, salty seawater floods the swamps and kills the trees.

HESSEL'S HAIRSTREAK

Hessel's hairstreak caterpillars must eat the leaves of the Atlantic cedar, a tree that grows in swamps along the Atlantic Ocean. But these trees are dying as seawater floods the land.

Right now, people are planting new trees, but that's a temporary solution. To save the swamps and everything living there, we need to stop global warming. If we make changes soon, we may be able to save Hessel's hairstreaks and many other creatures.

Burning oil, coal, and natural gas to heat homes and power cars causes global warming. When people use less of these fossil fuels, butterflies can live and grow.

To kill weeds, workers spray chemicals on golf courses, roadside ditches, and farmland. But these chemicals also harm the plants some caterpillars eat.

When people use these chemicals less often and raise the plants butterflies need
in protected places, butterflies can live and grow.

MONARCH

Monarch caterpillars only
eat one thing—milkweed, a
plant that grows in ditches or
at the edge of golf courses and
farmers' fields. When people
spray weed killer, the wind
blows the chemicals onto
milkweed. That's one reason
the number of monarchs has fallen as
much as 70 percent since 2012.
In some places, workers are now
using less weed killer. And people
are growing milkweed in yards
and nature centers. Hopefully,
it's not too late for monarchs.

Some caterpillars depend on plants that attack the trees people use to make paper.

THICKET HAIRSTREAK

Thicket hairstreak caterpillars must eat dwarf mistletoe, a plant that jams rootlike sinkers into trees and steals food and water. Dwarf mistletoe often attacks the large evergreen trees that grow in western forests.

For many years, forest rangers killed mistletoe because it was harming trees used to make paper and other wood products. But now they are letting it grow so that it can provide food and shelter for thicket hairstreak caterpillars and other forest creatures.

When people leave these plants alone, butterflies can live and grow.

Butterflies need more than just food to survive. They also need to stay safe and healthy. Some butterflies fly slowly and are easy to catch, so people like to collect them.

When people let these colorful insects fly free,
butterflies can live and grow.

UNCOMPAHGRE FRITILLARY

Uncompahgre fritillaries fly
slowly and stay close to the
ground. This makes them easy
to catch. And because they're
rare, some butterfly collectors
will pay more than $100 for
each one.

Now that Uncompahgre
fritillaries are on the
endangered species
list, it is against the law to
collect them. And park rangers have
rerouted trails away from their habitat.
Hopefully, these special butterflies
will be able to survive.

Some butterflies have trouble surviving when new plants invade the areas where they live.

When people choose native plants for their yards, butterflies can live and grow.

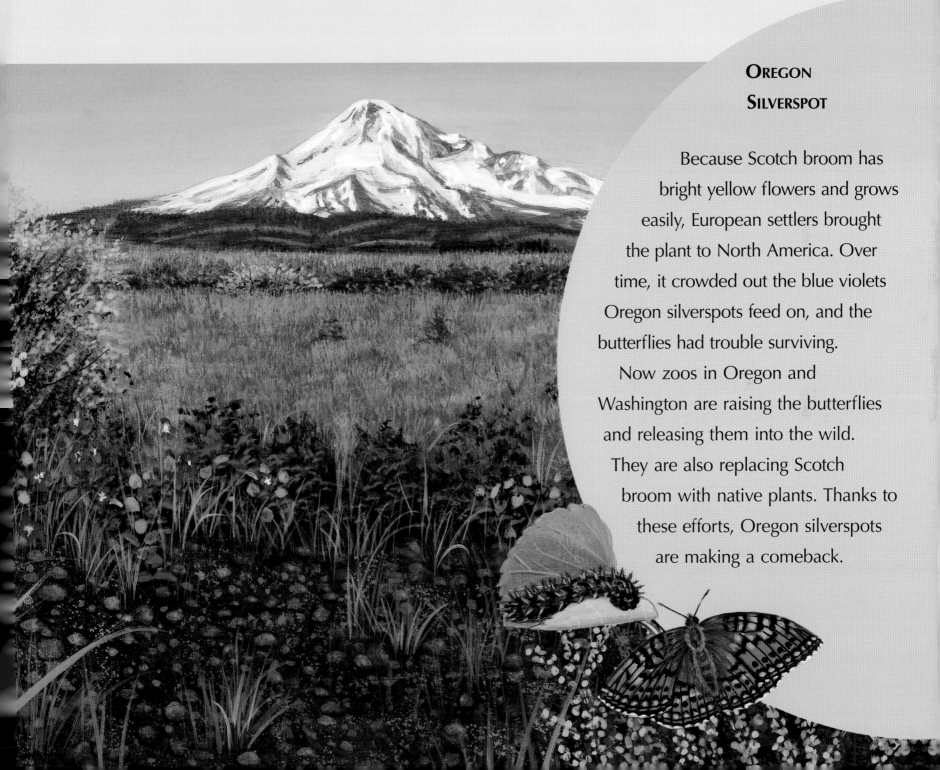

OREGON SILVERSPOT

Because Scotch broom has bright yellow flowers and grows easily, European settlers brought the plant to North America. Over time, it crowded out the blue violets Oregon silverspots feed on, and the butterflies had trouble surviving. Now zoos in Oregon and Washington are raising the butterflies and releasing them into the wild. They are also replacing Scotch broom with native plants. Thanks to these efforts, Oregon silverspots are making a comeback.

Butterflies have trouble surviving when their natural homes are destroyed. Some butterflies can only live in open fields.

HARRIS'S CHECKERSPOT

Not long ago, small family farms covered much of New England. But now, people are building houses and shopping malls on the land.

In Worcester, Massachusetts, the local electric company wanted to create new places for Harris's checkerspots to live. Workers often saw butterflies flitting along the grassy paths under power lines. They asked scientists when they could mow the grass without harming butterfly eggs or caterpillars. Now butterflies can spend their whole lives in these grassy places.

When people create new grassy areas, butterflies can live and grow.

Other butterflies can only survive in sandy thickets near the ocean.

When people restore and protect these wild places, butterflies can live and grow.

PALOS VERDES BLUE

Scientists thought Palos Verdes blue butterflies were extinct. But in 1994, about 100 were discovered on a Navy base in San Pedro, California. Scientists began raising butterflies in their labs, and people planted deerweed for the caterpillars to eat in the wild. Over time, more than 1,600 acres (647 hectares) of land have been set aside for the butterflies. Today, the number of Palos Verde blues is growing.

Many butterflies depend on wetland areas that are perfect for building homes and growing crops.

When people work to save these watery worlds, butterflies can live and grow.

MITCHELL'S SATYR

In the past, many of the grassy wetlands where Mitchell's satyrs live were drained to build homes. The land was used for farming too.

In 1992, the butterflies were added to the endangered species list. In 2006, people began restoring some wetlands. They also converted unused land into the perfect butterfly habitat. Each year, more and more Mitchell's satyrs have a place to call home.

When too many butterflies die, other living things may also have trouble surviving.

PLANTS NEED BUTTERFLIES

As a butterfly feeds on flower nectar, it becomes dusted with pollen. When the insect flies to another flower, the pollen goes along for the ride. At the next stop, some pollen falls off the butterfly's body and lands on the flower. Then the plant can use material in the pollen to make seeds, which will grow into new plants. Butterflies and moths pollinate more plants than any other insect, except bees. Without butterflies, some flowering plants might disappear from Earth forever.

That's why it's so important to protect butterflies and the places where they live.

OTHER ANIMALS NEED BUTTERFLIES

Butterflies are an important part of the food chain. Caterpillars rarely gobble up enough leaves to kill a plant. As they eat, their droppings fall to the ground and add nutrients to the soil. Both caterpillars and chrysalises are good sources of food for other insects as well as mice, opossums, skunks, birds, and toads. Adult butterflies are often eaten by spiders, dragonflies, and praying mantises. Without butterflies, many other creatures would go hungry.

Butterflies have lived on Earth for 140 million years.

STARTING A BUTTERFLY GARDEN

If every neighborhood had one or two butterfly gardens, many more butterflies would have everything they need to survive. There are plenty of great books that can help you begin a butterfly garden. To get started, you'll need a water supply and a variety of plants that bloom throughout the spring, summer, and early autumn. Ask the workers at a local garden center which plants the butterflies in your area like best.

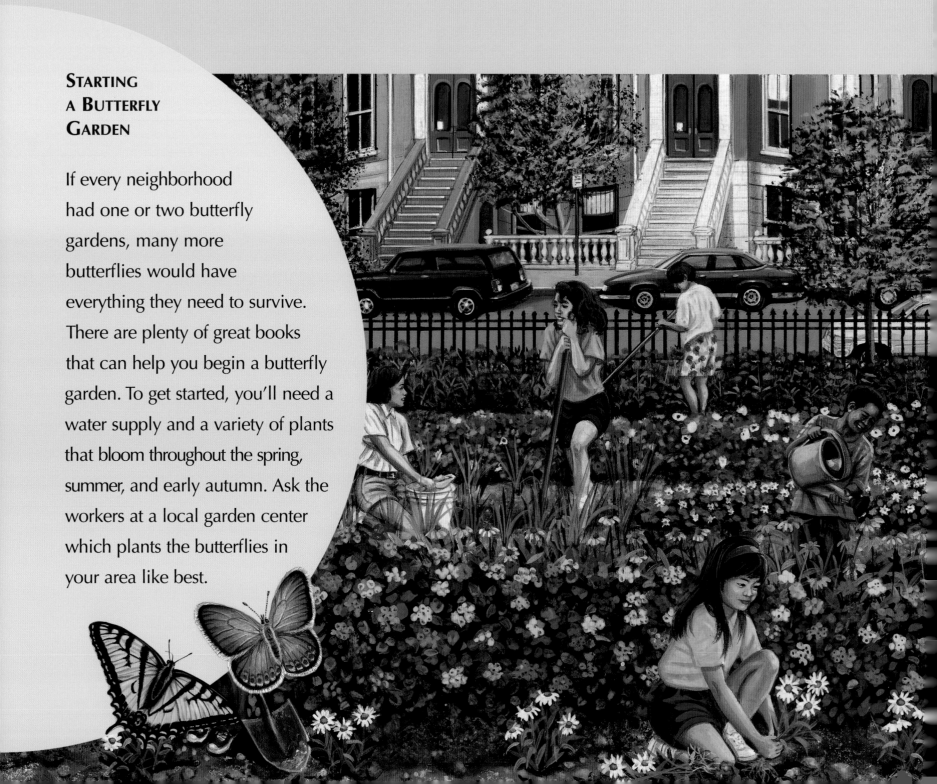

Some of the things people do can harm butterflies. But there are many ways you can help these special insects live far into the future.

HELPING BUTTERFLIES

* Do not catch and keep butterflies.
* Do not spray chemicals that could harm butterflies.
* Join a group of people that is keeping track of butterflies in your area.
* Write an article about butterflies for your school newspaper.
* Start a butterfly garden in your yard or neighborhood.

Butterfly Facts

✳ No one knows exactly how many kinds of butterflies live on Earth. So far, scientists have discovered more than 17,500 different species. About 750 kinds of butterflies live in North America.

✳ The Queen Alexandra's birdwing is the world's largest butterfly. Its wings stretch wider than the pages in this book. But the tiny pygmy blue butterfly is about the size of your thumbnail.

✳ Most adult butterflies live less than two weeks, but monarchs and mourning cloaks can live up to ten months.

✳ Some adult butterflies migrate when the days grow chilly. Other adult butterflies hibernate. Many butterflies spend the winter as eggs, caterpillars, or pupae.

✳ Butterflies have all kinds of tricks for protecting themselves from enemies. Can you guess why most predators stay away from the larva of eastern tiger swallowtails? Because their bodies look just like bird poop.

SELECTED SOURCES

"10,000 Acres of Atlantic White Cedar Forests to Be Restored in Pinelands." *NJ Spotlight News*, October 12, 2021. https://www.njspotlightnews.org/2021/10/nj-restoring-10000-acres-atlantic-white-cedar-ghost-forests-saltwater-climate-change-threatened.

Alexander, Kevin, Professor of Biology and Associate Vice President in Academic Affairs, Western Colorado University, Gunnison, Colorado, personal correspondence, October 3, 2022.

BugGuide. http://bugguide.net

Hixon, Michael. "Palos Verdes Peninsula Land Conservancy Adds Nearly 100 Acres for Wildlife Corridor." *The Orange County Register*, August 25, 2022. https://www.ocregister.com/2022/08/25/palos-verdes-peninsula-land-conservancy-adds-nearly-100-acres-for-wildlife-corridor/.

Opler, Paul. *Peterson First Guide to Butterflies and Moths*. Boston: Houghton Mifflin, 1998.

Wagenaar, Brian. "Science at Western: Andrea Williams Studies the Endangered Uncompahgre Fritillary Butterfly." *Top O' the World*, August 28, 2022. https://topotheworld.org/science-at-western-andrea-williams-studies-the-endangered-uncompahgre-fritillary-butterfly/.

Wheatley, Mason. "Karner Blue Butterfly Recovery in New Hampshire." U.S. Fish & Wildlife Service. https://www.fws.gov/story/karner-blue-butterfly-recovery-new-hampshire/.

RECOMMENDED FOR YOUNG READERS

Aston, Dianna Hutts. *A Butterfly Is Patient*. San Francisco: Chronicler Books, 2011.

Davidson, Laura. *Butterflies for Kids: A Junior Scientist's Guide to the Butterfly Life Cycle and Beautiful Species to Discover*. New York: Rockridge Press, 2021.

North American Butterfly Association. http://naba.org

Sayre, April Pulley. *Touch a Butterfly: Wildlife Gardening with Kids*. Boston: Shambala Publications, 2013.

Simon, Seymour. *Butterflies*. New York: HarperCollins, 2011.

ACKNOWLEDGMENTS

The author wishes to thank Brian Cassie of the North American Butterfly Association, Chris Leahy and Gail Howe of the Massachusetts Audubon Society, and David Wagner of the University of Connecticut at Storrs for their help in conceptualizing and preparing the manuscript. Thomas Emmel and Jaret Daniels of the University of Florida at Gainesville and Rudi Mattoni of the University of California in Los Angeles took time out of their busy schedules to discuss the endangered butterfly species they are studying.

The United States Geological Survey kindly provided range and habitat data for most of the butterflies mentioned in this book.

The illustrator gratefully acknowledges Daniel Soyka Beran, Jaret Daniels, Michael Durham and the Oregon Zoo, Paul Opler, and Larry West, who supplied photos used as reference for many of the illustrations in this book.

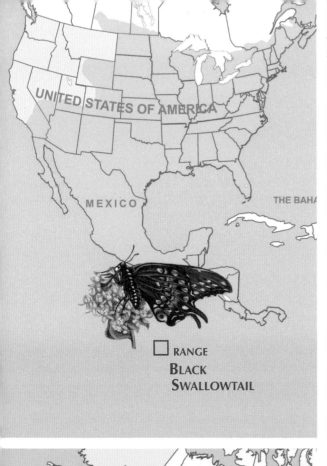

☐ RANGE
BLACK SWALLOWTAIL

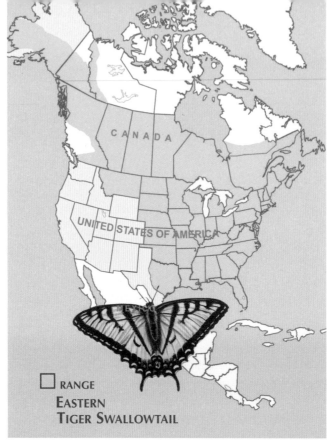

☐ RANGE
EASTERN TIGER SWALLOWTAIL

☐ RANGE
MOURNING CLOAK

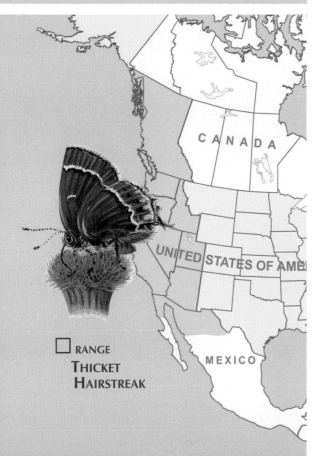

☐ RANGE
THICKET HAIRSTREAK

☐ RANGE
UNCOMPAHGRE FRITILLARY

☐ RANGE
OREGON SILVERSPOT